Mechanic Mike's Machines

Farm Machinery

A⁺

Smart Apple Media

Published by Smart Apple Media, an imprint of Black Rabbit Books
P.O. Box 3263, Mankato, Minnesota 56002
www.blackrabbitbooks.com

Produced by David West 👥 Children's Books
7 Princeton Court, 55 Felsham Road, London SW15 1AZ

Designed and illustrated by David West

Copyright © 2014 David West Children's Books

Library of Congress Cataloging-in-Publication Data

West, David, 1956-
Farm machinery / David West.
     pages cm. – (Mechanic Mike's machines)
 ISBN 978-1-62588-056-7 (library binding)
 ISBN 978-1-62588-095-6 (paperback)
1. Agricultural machinery–Juvenile literature. I. Title. II. Series: West, David, 1956- Mechanic Mike's machines.
 S675.25.W47 2015
 631.3–dc23

                            2013032023

Printed in China
CPSIA compliance information: DWCB14CP
010114

9 8 7 6 5 4 3 2 1

Mechanic Mike says:
This little guy will tell you something more about the machine.

 Find out what type of engine drives the machine.

 Discover something you didn't know.

 When was it invented or who invented it?

 What did we do before it was invented?

 Get your amazing fact here!

Contents

Mechanic Mike says:
Most tractors have a power take-off shaft at the back. This enables the farmer to transfer power from the tractor's engine to a towed machine, such as a baler or mower.

4

Tractor

The main work horse on the farm is the tractor. They are used for a variety of jobs such as pulling trailers, cultivators, planters, and balers. The engine provides power to all of the four large wheels to give extra grip.

The largest tractor is the Challenger's MT975B. It weighs just over 27 tons (24.49 tonnes).

The first tractors appeared around 1850. They were steam-powered plowing engines. In 1892, John Froelich invented and built the first gas-powered tractor in Iowa, USA.

Did you know that Henry Ford introduced the Fordson, the first mass-produced tractor, in 1917?

Before tractors were invented the work was done by oxen and large, powerful horses.

Modern farm tractors usually use **diesel engines**.

Mechanic Mike says:
Modern cultivators are used
after the soil has been plowed.

Cultivator

Fields are prepared for planting
with a cultivator. It is towed
behind a tractor. The disks and spiked
wheels turn the soil, getting air into it,
and pulling up weeds.

6

Cultivators can vary greatly in width, from 10 feet (3 m) to 80 feet (24 m) wide.

Oxen-drawn plowing was used by the Ancient Egyptians, over 3,000 years ago.

Did you know that deep plowing contributed to the destruction of the American and Canadian prairie lands in the 1930s? It was called the "Dust Bowl."

In ancient times, soil preparation was done by hand, with hoes and plows. Early plows and cultivators were originally drawn by animals such as horses, mules, or oxen.

Cultivators are powered by the tractor's engine via a power take-off shaft.

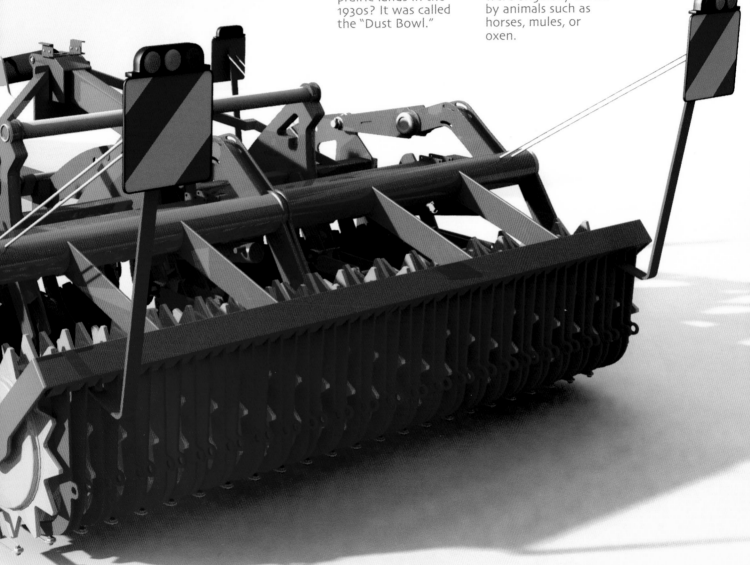

Mechanic Mike says:
Broadcast spreaders
scatter seeds. They are
not used for planting in
defined rows.

Spreader

This machine is used for spreading seeds or fertilizer. Seeds or pellets of fertilizer are dropped onto spinning disks, which scatter them onto the soil.

Large broadcast spreader units can spread widths of up to 90 feet (27 m).

 Did you know that there are some spreaders made for garden-size tractors that use a 12-volt motor to spin the dispersing disk?

 Mechanical spreaders were invented at the turn of the 20th century.

 Seeds used to be spread by hand as the farmer walked up and down a field.

 Broadcast spreaders are powered by the tractor's engine via a power take-off shaft.

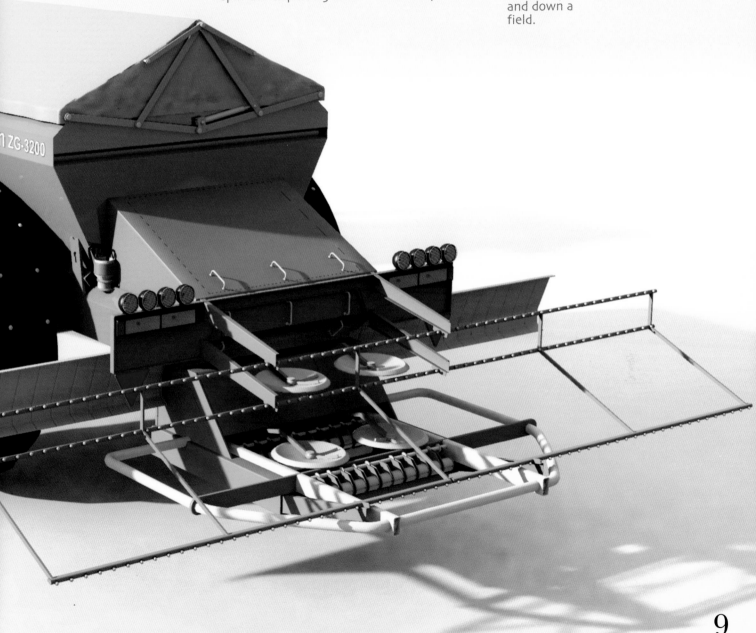

Planter

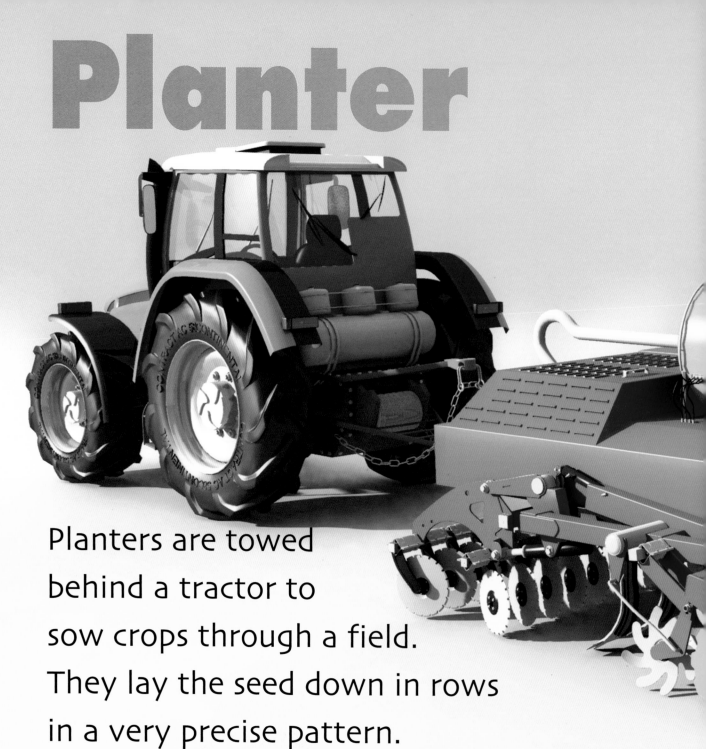

Planters are towed
behind a tractor to
sow crops through a field.
They lay the seed down in rows
in a very precise pattern.

Planters vary greatly in size, from 2 rows to the biggest in the world, which has 48 rows.

Henry Blair invented the seed planter in 1834, which allowed farmers to plant more corn using less labor in less time. The wheeled machine was pulled by a horse.

Before the invention of the seed planter the farmer had to plant the seeds by hand.

Did you know satellite navigation and automatic steering for the tractor are often used to make sure the seeds are planted accurately?

Planters are powered by the tractor's engine via a power take-off shaft.

Mechanic Mike says:
Planting machines such as rice planters take the back-breaking work out of the process. But there are still many places where it is done by hand.

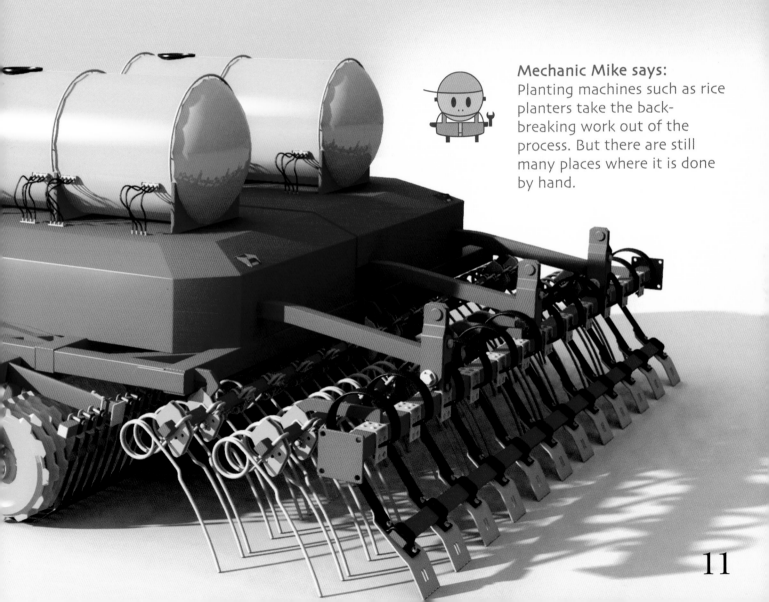

Harvester

This combine harvester is one of many different types of harvesters. It combines the three separate operations of reaping, threshing, and winnowing, into one process.

Mechanic Mike says:
First, the combine cuts the crop (reaping). Secondly, it loosens the edible part of the grain or seeds from the rest of the plant (threshing). Thirdly, it separates the grain or seeds from the husks and straw (winnowing).

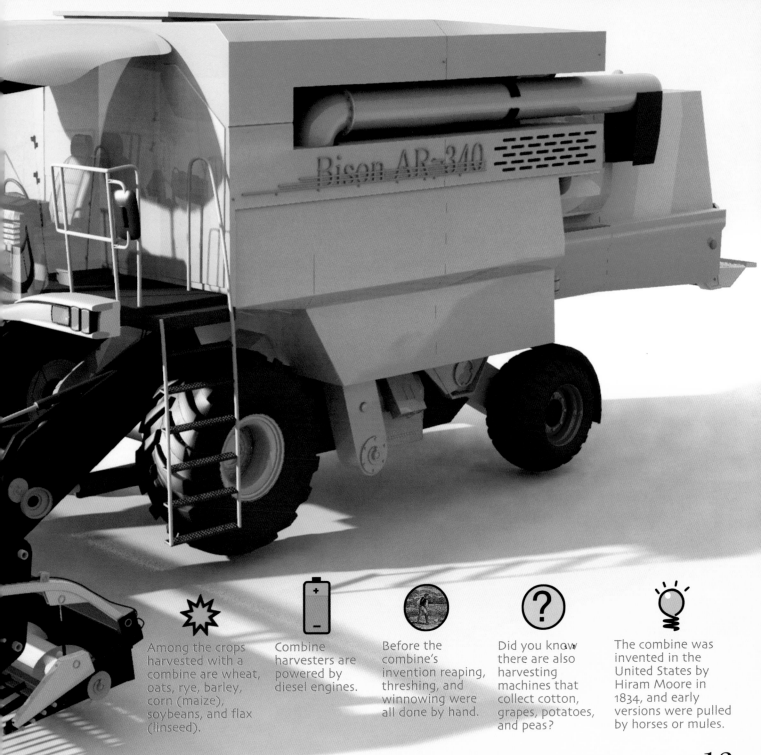

Among the crops harvested with a combine are wheat, oats, rye, barley, corn (maize), soybeans, and flax (linseed).

Combine harvesters are powered by diesel engines.

Before the combine's invention reaping, threshing, and winnowing were all done by hand.

Did you know there are also harvesting machines that collect cotton, grapes, potatoes, and peas?

The combine was invented in the United States by Hiram Moore in 1834, and early versions were pulled by horses or mules.

13

Grain carts can carry around 33,000 pounds (15 tonnes). The largest can carry 110,231 pounds (50 tonnes). That's the weight of about 25 cars!

Wagons have been used to carry grain since ancient times.

Grain was originally collected in bags weighing 240 pounds (109 kg). These would be lifted by hand on to a horse-drawn cart.

Did you know grain carts are also called grain wagons? They allow the harvester to operate continually, without the need for stopping to unload.

If the grain cart has an **auger**, it is powered by the tractor via a power take-off shaft.

Mechanic Mike says:
Grain carts are used to transport the grain or corn over fields from a combine harvester to a semi-trailer truck, which is used to cover larger distances by road.

14

Grain Cart

As the combine moves along it is accompanied by a grain cart, pulled by a tractor. The grain from the combine is poured into the cart using an auger.

Baler

After the harvester has finished, the leftover stalks lying on the ground are collected and compressed into bales of hay, and bound with twine.

Rectangular bales are easier to transport and don't roll away on hillsides.

Did you know some hay is stored in silos? This hay is much wetter than hay bales and turns to silage. Silage is used as food for cattle.

In 1872, a reaper that used a knotter device to bundle and bind hay was invented by Charles Withington.

Before the 19th century, hay was cut by hand and most typically stored in haystacks.

Balers are powered by the tractor's engine via a power take-off shaft.

Stacker

Bales of hay are picked up from the field and stacked onto trailers by a self-powered machine called a bale stacker.

Mechanic Mike says:
The pallet fork at the front of the stacker's arm can be swapped for other devices, such as a feed bucket, to allow it to perform other tasks.

Some balers use an automated device that throws the hay bale into the wagon behind it.

Automated devices for stacking bales as they exit the baler have been used for a few decades.

Before automated devices, teams of workers with a flatbed wagon would come by and use a sharp metal hook to grab the bale and throw it up onto the wagon. An assistant stacked the bales.

Did you know weights have to be added to the back of the stacker to stop it tipping forward when lifting heavy loads?

Bale stackers are powered by diesel engines.

Mechanic Mike says:
The front arm crops hay from bales. Augers carry the hay up the arm into the mixer. Here it is mixed with protein supplements, minerals, and vitamins to make the **Total Mixed Ration.**

The Total Mixed Ration is distributed from a side chute as the machine drives along the feed lot.

? Computers control the mixing of the Total Mixed Ration.

The self-propelled mixer feeder was invented in the 1980s.

Before automated mixers, cattle feed was mixed by hand.

Mixer

This strange machine is used for accurately weighing, mixing, and distributing measured rations for cattle.

Mixer wagons are powered by diesel engines.

Transportation

Farmers use special vehicles to carry themselves and their animals. **4X4** pickup trucks are used to get around, and to tow small trailers such as horse trailers.

Mechanic Mike says:
Pickup trucks are an ideal form of transportation on large farms as they can travel on roads and over rough terrain. Their open cargo area can carry bales of hay or small machines, as well as farm dogs.

Horses are carried to events in special horse trailers. Cattle and sheep are transported in special wagons pulled by trucks.

The first pickup was produced in 1925. It was based on the Ford Model T car, with a modified rear body.

Before these machines were invented, farmers got around their farms on horseback. Animals were driven to markets on foot.

Did you know some farmers use small **ATV**s to get around their farms?

Many pickup trucks have diesel engines.

Glossary

4x4
A vehicle that has four wheels powered by the engine instead of only two.

ATV
All Terrain Vehicles look like four-wheeled motorcycles. They are used off road by farmers and in sport.

auger
A conveyor that uses a large rotating screw to move material uphill.

diesel engine
An engine that uses diesel rather than gas for fuel.

Total Mixed Ration
The weighed and blended feed that make a complete ration of food for cows.

Index